UNDERSTANDING
The Bible

The Bible For Today

By the same author

OTHER BOOKS IN THIS SERIES

UNDERSTANDING
The Bible

The Bible For Today

by   John R. W. Stott

Understanding the Bible

SCRIPTURE UNION
47 Marylebone Lane
London W1M 6AX

Published in the United States by
Regal Books Division, G/L Publications
Glendale, California 91209   U.S.A.

Illustrations by Annie Valloton

Printed in Great Britain by
McCorquodale (Newton) Ltd., Newton-le-Willows

PUBLISHER'S PREFACE

UNDERSTANDING THE BIBLE has appeared in several editions, not only in the United Kingdom, North America, Australia and India, but in such languages as German, Swedish, Dutch, Spanish, Faroese, Japanese, Chinese and Thai. The author's objectives set out in his preface are being steadily fulfilled.

Now we are issuing the original publication in five separate volumes in a further attempt to achieve those aims. We anticipate meeting an even wider need; making readily available to new readers the individual subjects on which the Rev. John R. W. Stott has written so clearly.

Their use will not be confined to the individual reader; it will be practicable to use them in study and house groups, etc.

Each book contains recommendations for further reading and an index of scripture references referred to in the text.

PREFACE

Every author owes it to the reading public to explain himself. Why has he thought fit to swell the torrent of books—especially religious books—which pours from the world's printing presses every day? Can he justify his rash enterprise? Let me at least tell you frankly the kind of people I have had in mind while writing. They fall into two categories.

First, the new Christian. With the spread of secularism in our day, an increasing number of people are being added to Christ and His Church who have no religious background whatever. Here, for example, is a young man from a non-Christian family. The Christian instruction he received at school was minimal, and possibly misleading. In any case the fashion was to pay no attention to it. He did not go to Sunday School as a kid, and he has seldom if ever been to church. But now he has found Christ, or rather been found by Him. He is told he must read the Bible daily if he is to grow into spiritual maturity. The Bible is a closed book to him, however—an unexplored, uncharted territory. Who wrote it, he asks, and when, where and why? What is its message? What is the foundation for its claim to be a 'holy' or special book, the book of God? And how is it to be read and interpreted? These are proper questions to ask, and some answer must be given to them before the new Christian can derive maximum benefit from his Bible reading.

Then, secondly, there is the Christian of several years' standing. In the main, he has been a conscientious Bible reader. He has read his portion faithfully every day. But somehow it has become a stale habit. The years have passed, and he himself has changed and matured as a person. Yet he has not developed as a Christian in any comparable way. A sign (and cause) of this is that he still reads the Bible as he did when he was a child, or a new convert. Now he is tired of his superficiality, his immaturity, and not a little ashamed. He longs to become an adult, integrated Christian, who knows and pleases God, fulfils himself in serving others and can commend the gospel in meaningful terms to a lost, bewildered generation.

My desire is to assure such a Christian that the secrets of Christian maturity are ready to be found in Scripture by all who seek them. There is a breadth to God's Word which few of us ever encompass, a depth which we seldom plumb.

In particular, our Christianity is mean because our Christ is mean. We impoverish ourselves by our low and paltry views of Him. Some speak of Him today as if He were a kind of syringe to be carried about in our pocket, so that when we are feeling depressed we can give ourselves a fix and take a trip into fantasy. But Christ cannot be used or manipulated like that. The contemporary Church seems to have little understanding of the greatness of Jesus Christ as lord of creation and lord of the Church, before whom our place is on our faces in the dust. Nor do we seem to see His victory as the New Testament portrays it, with all things under His feet, so that if we are joined to Christ, all things are under our feet as well.

It seems to me that our greatest need today is an enlarged vision of Jesus Christ. We need to see Him as the One in whom alone the fulness of God dwells and in whom alone we can come to fulness of life.[1]

There is only one way to gain clear, true, fresh, lofty views of Christ, and that is through the Bible. The Bible is the prism by which the light of Jesus Christ is broken into its many and beautiful colours. The Bible is the portrait of Jesus Christ. We need to gaze upon Him with such intensity of desire that (by the gracious work of the Holy Spirit) He comes alive to us, meets with us, and fills us with Himself.

In order to apprehend Jesus Christ in His fulness, it is essential to understand the setting within which God offers Him to us. God gave Christ to the world in a specific geographical, historical and theological context. More simply, He sent Him to a particular place (Palestine), at a particular time (the climax of centuries of Jewish history) and within a particular framework of truth (progressively revealed and permanently recorded in the Bible). So the following chapters are concerned with the geography, history, theology, authority and interpretation of the Bible. Their object is to present the setting within which God once revealed and now offers Christ, so that we may the better grasp for ourselves and share with others the glorious fulness of Jesus Christ Himself.

NOTE

1 See Col. 1.19; 2.9, 10

THE BIBLE FOR TODAY

I once heard Dr. Alan Cole, of Sydney, remark that, surprising as it may seem, God sometimes blesses 'a poor exegesis of a bad translation of a doubtful reading of an obscure verse of a minor prophet'!

This is true. He does. But it gives us no possible excuse for slovenliness in Biblical interpretation. On the contrary, if the Bible is indeed God's word written, we should spare no pains and grudge no effort to discover what He has said (and says) in Scripture.

How then shall the student of the Bible grasp its message with accuracy? Where is he to look for help? Perhaps we should begin our answer by warning the reader against any pretension to infallibility. God's word is infallible, for what He has said is true. But no Christian individual, group or church has ever been or will ever be an infallible interpreter of God's word. Human interpretations belong to the sphere of tradition, and an appeal may always be made against tradition to the Scripture itself which tradition claims to interpret.

Nevertheless, God has made provision for us to grow in our understanding of the truth and to be protected from the worst forms of misinterpretation. He has given us three teachers to instruct us, and three principles to guide us.

The Enlightenment of the Holy Spirit

Our foremost teacher is the Holy Spirit Himself. 'Hermeneutics' is the technical name given to the science of interpreting Scripture, and it should be obvious that a truly Biblical hermeneutic will be consistent with the nature of the Bible itself. If, then, the Biblical authors spoke from God, not on their own impulse but as they were moved by the Holy Spirit,[1] it is the Holy Spirit who can interpret what He caused them to speak. The best interpreter of every book is its author, since He alone knows what He intended to say. So God's book can be interpreted by God's Spirit alone.

The work of the Holy Spirit in communicating God's truth to man is now seen to have two stages. The first and objective stage is 'revelation', the disclosure of the truth in Scripture. The second and subjective stage may be called 'illumination', the enlightenment of our minds to comprehend the truth disclosed in Scripture. Each process is indispensable. Without revelation we have no truth to perceive; without illumination no faculty with which to perceive it.

An illustration comes from the days of Isaiah when, in judgment upon His rebellious people, God ceased to speak to them. His truth became like a sealed book, and His people like illiterate children. There were thus two barriers to their receiving His word:

'When men give it to one who can read, saying "Read this", he says, "I cannot, for it is sealed". And when they give the book to one who cannot read, saying "Read this", he says, "I cannot read."' (Is. 29. 11, 12)

Once we grant the necessity of the Holy Spirit's illumination before we can understand God's word, we are ready to consider the kind of people the Holy Spirit enlightens.

First, the Holy Spirit enlightens the regenerate. An experience of rebirth is essential before we are able to grasp heavenly truth. 'Unless one is born anew', Jesus said, 'he cannot see the kingdom of God'.[3] This fact the apostle Paul echoed:

'The unspiritual man (the "natural" or "unregenerate" man) does not receive the gifts of the Spirit of God, for they are folly to him, and he is not able to understand them because they are spiritually discerned.'[4]

Many have borne witness to this out of their own experience. For example, William Grimshaw, one of the leading English evangelicals in the eighteenth century, said to a friend after his conversion that 'If God had drawn up His Bible to heaven, and sent him down another, it would not have been newer to him.'[5]

I can myself testify to something very similar. My mother brought me up to read a passage of the Bible every day. For her sake and out of habit I continued the practice until my later teens. But it was a largely meaningless routine, for I did not understand what I was reading. After my conversion, however, the Bible immediately began to become a living book to me. I am not of course claiming that I suddenly understood it all. Nor do I pretend that I no longer found some of it dull and difficult. But it assumed a new relevance for me, as the Holy Spirit illumined and applied its message to my life.

3

Secondly, the Holy Spirit enlightens the humble. There is no greater hindrance to understanding than pride, and no more essential condition than humility. Jesus put the matter beyond dispute:

'I thank Thee, Father, Lord of heaven and earth, that Thou hast hidden these things from the wise and understanding and revealed them to babes; yea, Father, for such was Thy gracious will.'[6]

The 'wise and understanding' from whom God hides himself are the intellectually proud, and 'babes' the humble and sincere. It is not the ignorance or even the simplicity of a child which Jesus commended, but its open, receptive and unprejudiced approach. It is to such only that God reveals Himself. As Charles Simeon wrote:

'In the beginning of my enquiries I said to myself, I am a fool; of that I am quite certain. One thing I know assuredly, that in religion of myself I know nothing. I do not therefore sit down to the perusal of Scripture in order to impose a sense on the inspired writers; but to receive one, as they give it me. I pretend not to teach them, I wish like a child to be taught by them.'[7]

There is only one way to express such an attitude of humble expectancy before God, and that is by prayer. We need both to pray before we read Scripture and to read it in a prayerful frame of mind, and many Christians have found it helpful to use some of the Bible's own prayers for illumination. For example, the Psalmist's petition:

'Open my eyes, that I may behold wondrous things out of thy law.'[8]

Or one of Paul's great prayers, in all of which he asks in some way for an increase of knowledge or under-standing. For example:

4

'. . . That the God of our Lord Jesus Christ, the Father of glory, may give you a spirit of wisdom and of revelation in the knowledge of Him, having the eyes of your hearts enlightened, that you may know what is the hope to which He has called you, what are the riches of His glorious inheritance in the saints, and what is the immeasurable greatness of His power in us who believe . . .'.[9]

Such a humbling of ourselves before God, acknowledging our darkness and appealing for His enlightenment, will not go unrewarded. Not long after his conversion at Pembroke College, Oxford, George Whitefield wrote in his journal:

'I began to read the Holy Scriptures upon my knees, laying aside all other books, and praying over, if possible, every line and word. This proved meat indeed and drink indeed to my soul. I daily received fresh life, light and power from above.'[10]

Thirdly, the Holy Spirit enlightens the obedient. This is much emphasized. Since God's purpose through Scripture is not merely to 'instruct' in general terms but specifically 'to instruct you for salvation'.[11] He is concerned about the response which readers give to His word. And the degree of our responsiveness, of our willingness to hear and obey, will to a large extent determine the degree of understanding we receive. Thus Jesus promised that those who have a will to do God's will would know whether His teaching was true, and that He would show Himself personally to those who prove their love for Him by their obedience.[12] Conversely, it is those who violate their conscience by disobedience who make shipwreck of their faith.[13] Nobody who does not practise what he already knows can expect to advance in his knowledge.

Fourthly, the Holy Spirit enlightens the communicative. The understanding He gives us is not intended for our private enjoyment alone; it is given us to be shared with others. We hold it on trust. A lamp is not brought into a room to be put under a bed, Jesus said, but on a stand. In the same way He intended His teaching to be made known, not to be kept secret. The apostles were to take heed what and how they heard. They were to listen to their Master's teaching, in order to communicate it. Otherwise, they would not receive any more:

'The measure you give will be the measure you get, and still more will be given you.'[14]

The Christian's Disciplined Study

If the Holy Spirit is our first and foremost teacher, there is a sense in which we ourselves, in our very dependence on the Spirit, must also teach ourselves. That is to say, in the process of divine education we are not wholly passive, but are expected to use our own reason responsibly. For in our reading of Scripture divine illumination is no substitute for human endeavour. Nor is humility in seeking light from God alone inconsistent with the most disciplined industry in study.

Scripture itself lays great stress on the conscientious Christian use of the mind, not of course in order to stand in judgment on God's word, but rather in order to submit to it, to grapple with it, to understand it and to relate it to the contemporary scene. Indeed, there are frequent complaints in Scripture that man keeps forgetting his basic rationality as a human being made in God's image and behaves instead 'like a horse or a mule, without understanding'.[15]

So Jesus rebuked His apostles for their lack of understanding and their failure to use their common sense.[16] He reproached the multitudes similarly:

'Why do you not judge for yourselves what is right?'[17]

This command to 'judge for yourselves' is particularly prominent in Paul's first letter to Corinth. Here was a church which laid claim to great wisdom, but failed to exhibit it. Again and again Paul asks incredulously 'Do you not know. . . .?'[18] and introduces his apostolic instruction with formulae like 'I want you to know, brethren' or 'I do not want you to be uninformed'.[19] He is clear that, whereas the natural or unregenerate man is unable to understand God's truth, the spiritual or regenerate man 'judges all things'. That is, what the natural man cannot discern, the spiritual man can and does, because he is inhabited and ruled by the Holy Spirit and so has 'the mind of Christ'.[20]

This conviction leads Paul, in this same Corinthian letter, to appeal to his readers' reason. He writes:

'I speak as to sensible men; judge for yourselves what I say'.[21]

In other New Testament letters similar exhortations occur. Christians are to 'test the spirits' (i.e. human teachers claiming divine inspiration) and indeed to 'test everything' they hear.[22] Again, when faced with difficult ethical decisions, they are to give their minds to the problem, so that each may be 'fully convinced in his own mind'.[23] It is a mark of Christian maturity to have our 'faculties trained by practice to distinguish good from evil.'[24]

We must, then, take seriously this Biblical injunction to use our rational and critical powers. We are not to oppose prayer and thought as alternative means of increasing our understanding of Scripture, but to combine them. Daniel in the Old Testament and Paul in the New are good examples of this balance:

'Fear not, Daniel, for from the first day that you set

your mind to understand and humbled yourself before your God, your words have been heard. . . .'[25]

'Think over what I say, for the Lord will grant you understanding in everything.'[26]

It is not enough to humble ourselves before God and look to Him for understanding; we must also set our minds to understand Scripture and think over what is written in it. As Charles Simeon put it:

'For the attainment of divine knowledge, we are directed to combine a dependence on God's Spirit with our own researches. Let us, then, not presume to separate what God has thus united.'[27]

Sometimes our growth in understanding is inhibited by a proud and prayerless self-confidence, but at other times by sheer laziness and indiscipline. He who would increase in the knowledge of God must both abase himself before the Spirit of truth and commit himself to a lifetime of study.

The Teaching of the Church

Our third teacher is the Church. So far our portrayal of how God teaches His people from His word has been entirely individualistic. And it has been true. For it is God's loving purpose to enlighten, save, reform and nourish His people by His word as each hears it or reads it for himself. Our sixteenth-century reformers were quite right to want to translate the Bible into plain English and put it into the hands of plain people. For they were appalled at the widespread ignorance of Scripture. Hence William Tyndale's famous jibe to a clergyman critic:

'If God spare my life, ere many years pass I will cause a boy that driveth the plough shall know more of the Scriptures than thou dost.'[28]

We must also agree with the reformers' insistence on what they termed 'the right of private judgment', the birthright of every child of God to hear his Father's voice speaking to him directly through Scripture. This they asserted over against the claim of the Church of Rome that she had been given a unique 'magisterium' or teaching authority, because of which she alone could supply the true interpretation of Scripture.

Nevertheless, in rejecting every attempt to interpose the Church or any other authoritative teaching body between God and His people, we must not deny that the Church has a place in God's plan to give His people a right understanding of His word. The individual Christian's humble, prayerful, diligent and obedient study of Scripture is not the only way the Holy Spirit makes clear what He has revealed. It would hardly be humble to ignore what the Spirit may have shown to others. The Holy Spirit is indeed our teacher, but He teaches us indirectly through others as well as directly to our own minds. It was not to one man that He revealed the truths now enshrined in Scripture, but to a multiplicity of prophets and apostles; His work of illumination is given to many also. It is not as individuals merely, but 'with all the saints' that we are given 'power to comprehend . . . what is the breadth and length and height and depth, and to know the love of Christ which surpasses knowledge'.[29]

A recognition of this truth will give us more respect than we customarily have for 'tradition', that is, for the understanding of Biblical truth which has been handed down from the past to the present. Although the Holy Spirit's work of Biblical inspiration was unique, His teaching ministry did not cease when the last apostle died. It changed from revelation to illumination. Gradually and progressively over the centuries of Church history, the Spirit of truth enabled the Church to grasp, clarify and formulate the great doctrines of Scripture.

We owe much to the so-called Catholic Creeds ('catholic' because they were accepted by the whole Church) and Reformation confessions, together with the Biblical commentaries and theological treatises of individual scholars.

If we should not despise the heritage of the past, neither should we despise the teachers of the contemporary Church. The pastoral ministry is a teaching ministry, and 'pastors and teachers' are gifts which the ascended Christ still bestows upon His Church.[30] We should also be willing to listen to each other and learn from each other. The Holy Spirit can illumine our minds through group as well as individual Bible study. The apostle Paul clearly envisaged this kind of mutual instruction in the local church when he wrote:

'Let the word of Christ dwell in you richly, as you teach and admonish one another in all wisdom . . .'[31]

Luke gives a striking example of the role of the teacher in Acts 8.26–39. An Ethiopian minister of state, while travelling home from Jerusalem by chariot, was reading the prophecy of Isaiah. Philip the evangelist asked him: 'Do you understand what you are reading?' To which he replied: 'How can I, unless someone guides me?' So Philip went up to sit beside him and to explain the Scripture to him. Calvin comments:

'That is also why the reading of Scripture bears fruit with such a few people today, because scarcely one in a hundred is to be found who gladly submits himself to teaching. . . .

'Now if any of us is diffident about himself, but shows that he is teachable, angels will come down from heaven to teach us, rather than that the Lord allow us to labour in vain. However, following the example of the (Ethiopian) eunuch, we must make use of all the

10

aids which the Lord sets before us for the understanding of Scripture. Fanatics seek inspirations from heaven, and at the same time despise the minister of God, by whose hand they ought to have been ruled. Others, relying on their own penetrating insight, do not deign to hear anybody or to read any commentaries. But God does not wish the aids, which He appoints for us, to be despised, and does not allow contempt of them to go unpunished. And we must keep in mind here, that not only is Scripture given to us, but interpreters and teachers are also added to help us. That is why the Lord chose Philip for the eunuch, rather than an angel'.[32]

Of course no human teacher is infallible, either of the past or of the present, and Christ forbade us to give any human teacher a slavish following.[33] Ultimately, God Himself is our teacher and, speaking ideally, we may all be described as 'taught by God'.[34] Indeed, in principle, because of the apostolic word and the anointing Spirit given to us all, we 'have no need that anyone should teach' us.[35] The right of private judgment must not be taken away from us. Sometimes it is even necessary for us, out of loyalty to the plain meaning of Scripture, to disagree with teachers in the Church and say (I hope humbly):

'I have more understanding than all my teachers, for Thy testimonies are my meditation'.[36]

Nevertheless, I must repeat that God has appointed teachers in His Church. It is our Christian duty to listen to them with respect, humility and eagerness, and to feed upon God's word from their lips when they faithfully expound it, at the same time ourselves 'examining the Scriptures daily' to see if what they say is true.[37]

Our three teachers, then, whom I have mentioned are the Holy Spirit, ourselves and the Church. It is by receiving the illumination of the Spirit, by using our own reason and by listening to the teaching of others in the Church that we grow in our understanding of Scripture. I am anxious not to be misunderstood. I am emphatically not saying that Scripture, reason and tradition are a threefold authority of equal importance by which we come to know God's truth. No. Scripture alone is God's word written, and the Holy Spirit its ultimate interpreter. The place of the individual's reason and of the Church's tradition lies in the elucidation and application of Scripture. But both are subordinate to God Himself as He speaks to us through His word.

We turn now from the three teachers who instruct us to the three principles which are to guide us in our interpretation of Scripture.

It is often said by our critics, especially by those who know what a high view of Scripture we take, that 'you can make the Bible mean anything you like'. They are probably thinking of non-Christian and semi-Christian cults which support their particular opinions by an arbitrary selection and interpretation of proof texts. But the New Testament itself condemns those who 'tamper with God's word' and 'twist' it to suit their own purposes.[38] To those who accuse us of this, I always reply: 'You are quite right. You *can* make the Bible mean anything you like—if you are unscrupulous enough. But if you are scrupulously honest in your approach to the Bible and in your use of sound principles of interpretation, far from your being able to manipulate Scripture, you will find Scripture controlling and directing you'. What, then, are these sound principles of interpretation?

The Natural Sense

First, we must look for the *natural* sense. I will call this the principle of simplicity.

12

One of our basic Christian convictions is that 'God is light and in Him is no darkness at all.'[39] That is to say, it is as much the nature of God to reveal Himself as it is the nature of light to shine. Now God has revealed Himself chiefly by speaking. We may be quite sure, therefore, that He has spoken in order to be understood, and that He has intended Scripture (the record of the divine speech) to be plain to its readers. For the whole purpose of revelation is clarity not confusion, a readily intelligible message, not a set of dark and mysterious riddles.

This principle of simplicity strikes at the root of much popular interpretation. For example, the destructive criticism of radical Christians would limit the truth to a tiny minority of scholars who claim the competence to sift the wheat from the chaff in Scripture, while the fanciful reconstructions of some evangelical Christians would turn Scripture into a complicated jigsaw puzzle to which they alone possess the key. Over against these distortions we must assert that God's whole purpose in speaking and in causing His speech to be preserved is that He wanted to communicate to ordinary people and save them.

It is true that in some matters Scripture is not as plain as in others. This is apparent from the fact that, although devout and careful students of the Bible, deeply concerned to submit to its authority, enjoy a very wide measure of agreement on the great fundamentals of historic Christianity, they still disagree on some points. One thinks, for example, of such questions as these: whether baptism should be administered only to adult believers or to the children of Christian parents as well, and whether candidates should be immersed in the water or have it poured over them; whether our doctrine of the church should be 'independent' (each local church being autonomous) or 'connexional' (local churches being in some way federated); whether the ministry of the church should be episcopal or presbyterian, or indeed whether the local assembly should rather have a non-professional pastoral oversight; whether miracles (e.g. the instantaneous healing of organic diseases without medical means) should be expected in the contemporary church regularly, occasionally or never; and whether the 'millenium' (the reign of Christ for a thousand years) is intended to be understood literally as a future earthly event or symbolically as a present spiritual reality.

When equally Biblical Christians disagree in such matters, what should we do? We should be humble enough to re-examine them ourselves in the light of sound principles of interpretation. And we should be mature enough to discuss them with one another without rancour. If then we still disagree, we must regard such disputed points as being secondary in importance and respect one another with mutual Christian love and tolerance. We should also rejoice that in all the central doctrines of the faith we remain agreed, for in these the Scripture is plain, perspicuous and virtually self-interpreting.

God chose human language as the vehicle of His self-revelation. In speaking to men through men He used the language of men. As a result, although Scripture is unlike all other books in being the word of God, it is also like all other books in being the words of men. Since it is unique because divine, we must study it like no other book, praying to the Holy Spirit for illumination. Since it is ordinary because human, we must study it like every other book, paying attention to the common rules of vocabulary, grammar and syntax. For if (as we saw in the previous chapter) God did no violence to the agents of His revelation (human persons), He did no violence to the instrument either (human language).

It follows that no serious Bible reader can escape the discipline of linguistic study. Best of all would be a knowledge of the original languages, Hebrew and Greek.

But most will read in English, and for them an accurate modern version is essential. Although popular paraphrases are useful additional helps, there is no substitute for a careful, scholarly translation like the Revised Version or the Revised Standard Version, which (though both revisions of the Authorised Version) are probably still the best translations available in English. To-day's English Version also deserves a special mention, since it combines reliability with unusually simple and straightforward language. An analytical Concordance (like Young's or Strong's) is another extremely valuable tool, for it not only groups the Biblical words according to the English (AV) text but then subdivides them into the original Hebrew and Greek words and gives their meaning.

In reading the words and sentences of the Biblical text, we must look first of all for their obvious and natural meaning. In Sir Charles Odgers' standard book on the interpretation of legal deeds and documents his third rule is that 'words are to be taken in their literal meaning'. Unless the subject-matter shows otherwise, he writes, 'the plain, ordinary meaning of the words used is to be adopted in construing a document'.[40]

Unfortunately, the fanciful allegorization of Scripture has often brought serious Bible reading into disrepute. It was already indulged in by Jewish commentators before Christ, of whom Philo of Alexandria was the notorious example. It is not surprising that some Christian commentators in the post-apostolic period tried their hand at the same game. The so-called *Epistle of Barnabas*, for instance, an apocryphal work of (probably) the early second century A.D., contains some outrageous allegorizations. In one passage the author quotes the Mosaic regulation that the Jews might eat every animal that divides the hoof and chews the cud, and explains it thus:

'Cleave unto those that fear the Lord, . . . with those who know that meditation is a work of gladness and who chew the cud of the word of the Lord. But why that which divides the hoof? Because the righteous man both walks in this world and at the same time looks for the holy world to come'.[41]

Now certainly to 'chew the cud' of God's word is a very suggestive expression for Bible meditation, and also the Christian is a citizen of two worlds. But equally certainly this is not what Moses had in mind when he wrote about cud-chewing, cloven-hoofed animals!

The allegorical school of interpretation was further promoted by Origen of Alexandria in the fourth century A.D. and by medieval churchmen. It is greatly to the credit of the sixteenth century reformers that they rescued Scripture from this kind of arbitrary treatment and insisted that what is simple and straightforward is always to be preferred to subtleties. John Calvin put it admirably:

'Let us know, then, that the true meaning of Scripture is the natural and obvious meaning; and let us embrace and abide by it resolutely. Let us not only neglect as doubtful, but boldly set aside as deadly corruptions, those pretended expositions which lead us away from the natural meaning'.[42]

To look for the natural meaning of Scripture is not necessarily the same as looking for the literal meaning. For sometimes the natural meaning is figurative rather than literal. Jesus Himself had to reproach some of His hearers for their excessive literalism. Nicodemus misunderstood His reference to a second birth so completely that he asked incredulously whether a man can re-enter his mother's womb and be born. The Samaritan woman seems to have supposed that the living, thirst-quenching water which He offered her was down Jacob's well. And

16

when later Jesus claimed He could satisfy people's hunger by giving Himself to them as living bread, they asked 'how can this man give us His flesh to eat?'.[43] These examples should be enough to warn us against a dead and rigid literalism. It should have been obvious that Jesus was using figures of speech.

His favourite form of instruction was the parable, though occasionally He used the allegory. The difference between them is that in an allegory the similitude is drawn at many points, whereas the parable is an everyday story told to illustrate one main lesson, the wealth of detail being added not to teach subsidiary lessons but for dramatic effect. Examples of the allegory are the Good Shepherd in John 10, the Vine and the Branches in John 15 and the Sower in Mark 4. An example of the parable is the Good Samaritan.[44] Jesus told it in answer to the question 'Who is my neighbour?' and taught from it that true neighbour-love transcends the barriers of race and religion. It is not legitimate to press the details, e.g. to suggest that the inn represents the church and the two denarii given to the innkeeper the two sacraments. This would be to turn an obvious parable into an allegory and to provoke questions about what is represented by the brigands, the oil, the wine and the donkey!

Scripture is very rich in metaphorical language, and in every metaphor it is essential to ask at what point the analogy is being drawn. We must avoid arguing from analogy, that is, elaborating the correspondence beyond the limits which Scripture sets. Thus, God is our Father and we are His children. As our Father, He has begotten us, He loves us and cares for us. As His children, we depend on Him and must love and obey Him. But we have no liberty to argue, for example, that since God is our heavenly Father, we must also have a heavenly mother, on the ground that no child can have a father without a mother. Nor can we argue that because we are

17

called 'children', we can avoid the responsibility of adult thought and action. For the same Scripture which commends to us the humility of a little child also condemns in us a child's immaturity.

If some Scripture is literal and some figurative, how are we to tell which is which? The fundamental answer is that we are to look for the natural sense. Common sense will usually guide us. In particular, it is wise to ask ourselves what is the intention of the author or speaker. Let me give two examples.

First, it is often said that the Old Testament authors conceived the universe as a 'three-decker' construction with earth as man's dwelling-place, heaven above him like a great canopy punctured with holes through which the stars peeped, and *sheol* (the abode of the dead) beneath him; that they believed this in a literal and spatial way; and that when it rained, for instance, God had literally 'opened the windows of heaven'. I do not of course deny that this is the kind of language they used, but I do seriously doubt whether they believed it literally or intended their readers to understand it literally. Take Psalm 75. In verse 3 God is represented as saying that 'when the earth totters', it is He who 'keeps steady its pillars'. Did the psalmist think that the earth was literally balanced on stilts? I think not. In the next verse God commands the wicked 'do not lift up your horn' (a symbol of prosperity and success) and in verse 10 it is written that 'the horns of the wicked will be cut off', while in verse 8 we are told that in the Lord's hand 'there is a cup with foaming wine well mixed' (a symbol of His wrath). To me it is quite gratuitous to insist that the author thought the earth was set on literal pillars, unless we are prepared equally to insist that he thought the wicked have literal horns (which will one day be cut off) and that God holds a literal cup of foaming wine which He will one day pour out upon all the wicked of the earth.

My other example is taken from the special form of Biblical literature called 'apocalyptic', which claims to set forth hidden truths of both present reality and future history, usually in a series of weird and wonderful images. The Book of Revelation is a Christian apocalypse. In it God's redeemed people, gathered round His throne, are said to be wearing white robes which they have 'washed' ... and made ... white in the blood of the Lamb'.[45] Now to take this literally would be rather repulsive. It would also be impossible, since robes laundered in lamb's blood would not come out white. No. The author clearly intends the expression as a symbol to be interpreted, not as an image to be visualized. We are to understand that the righteousness of God's people (their 'white robes') is due entirely to the death of Christ ('the blood of the Lamb') in which they have put their trust ('washed their robes'). Thus, in this case too, the 'natural' sense is the figurative, not the literal.

The Original Sense

Secondly, we must look for the *original* sense of Scripture. This is the principle of history.

I have shown in Book 1 that God chose to reveal Himself in a precise historical context. Although His self-revelation is addressed to every man of every age and every country, each part of it was addressed in the first instance to a particular people of a particular age in a particular country. Therefore the permanent and universal message of Scripture can be understood only in the light of the circumstances in which it was originally given. It would obviously be very misleading to read back into Scripture the notions of a later age. As Charles Simeon wrote about the ideals of his preaching ministry:

'My endeavour is *to bring out of Scripture what is there, and not to thrust in what I think might be there. I*

19

have a great jealousy on this head; never to speak more or less than I believe the mind of the Spirit, in the passage I am expounding'.[46]

So, as we read the Bible, we need to keep asking ourselves: what did the author intend to convey by this? What is he actually asserting? What will his original hearers have understood him to have meant? This enquiry is commonly known as the 'grammatico-historical' method of interpretation. J. Gresham Machen has described it well:

'Scientific historical method in the interpretation of the Bible requires that the Biblical writers should be allowed to speak for themselves. A generation or so ago that feature of scientific method was exalted to the dignity of a principle, and was honoured by a long name. It was called "grammatico-historical exegesis". The fundamental notion of it was that the modern student should distinguish sharply between what he would have said or what he would have liked to have the Biblical writer say, and what the writer actually did say'.[47]

As we attempt to transport ourselves back into the author's mind and times, and to listen to his words as if we were among his first readers, we shall need particularly to consider the situation, the style and the language in which he wrote.

First, the situation. The proper function of literary and historical criticism is to reconstruct the *mise en scène* of the Biblical book in question. Who wrote it and to whom? In what circumstances? For what reason? Floods of light are thrown on the text of the Old Testament prophets, for example, if we can fit them into the story of Israel. The same is true of the New Testament epistles and the story of the early Church as Luke tells it in the Acts, and specially the missionary journeys of Paul. For example, Paul's *Letter to the Philippians* becomes a much more human document if on the one hand we can picture the author under house arrest in Rome (or possibly Ephesus) and on the other Lydia, the jailor and the slave-girl (whose conversions are described in Acts 16) as among its first readers.

A careful consideration of the historical background to the letters of Paul and James would have protected Luther from finding them contradictory and from rejecting James' letter as made of 'straw'. It is true that Paul declared a man 'justified by faith apart from works of law' and gave Abraham as an example,[48] whereas James declared a man 'justified by works and not by faith alone' and also quoted Abraham as an example.[49] But their positions are not mutually irreconcilable. Paul was tilting at legalists who believed in salvation by works, James at religionists who believed in salvation by orthodoxy. Both believed that salvation was by faith and that a saving faith would manifest itself in good works. It was natural in their particular circumstances, however, that Paul should stress the faith which issues in works, and James the works which spring from faith.

Secondly, the style. It is important to take note of the literary *genre* of each Biblical book. Is it prose or poetry, historical narrative or wisdom literature? Is it law, prophecy, psalm or apocalyptic? Is it a drama, or a letter, or that distinctively Christian form called a 'gospel', a collection of the words and deeds of Jesus which bear witness to Him? How we interpret what we read, not least whether we take it literally or figuratively, will depend largely on its form and style.

Thirdly, the language. All human language is a living, changing thing. The meaning of words alters from century to century and culture to culture. We cannot read the word 'love' in Scripture and immediately suppose we know what it means. Four different Greek words are used in the New Testament, all translated 'love' in English. But each has a distinctive meaning, and only one expresses what Christians mean by love, which is poles apart from the erotica of twentieth-century glossy magazines.

For many centuries scholars were not able to recognize the kind of Greek in which the New Testament was written. It was neither classical Greek nor modern Greek. Some thought it was made up specially for the purpose. They even called it 'the language of the Holy Ghost'. But towards the close of the last century, in the dry sands of Egypt, archaeologists began to discover large quantities of ancient papyrus rolls. They were mostly secular and non-literary documents. Many had come from the waste paper baskets of public record offices, whose contents had been dumped on the local rubbish heap. And their Greek (the *koinē* or common language of every day) was found to be largely the same as that of the New Testament. So now the meaning of New Testament Greek words has to be sought against a background not only of classical Greek and of Hebrew thought but also of the secular language of the day. I will give one example only.

In his two letters to the Thessalonians Paul several times refers to those he describes as *ataktos*. In classical Greek the word was commonly used of soldiers who broke rank, of an army in disarray. So the Authorized Version translates the word 'disorderly', and it was assumed that there was an undisciplined group of some kind in the Thessalonian church. But two or three apprenticeship contracts were discovered among the papyri which contain an undertaking that should the boy play truant from work or exceed his annual holiday, the lost time would be made good. And the word for playing truant is *ataktos*, or rather its cognate verb. So the Revised Standard Version renders it not 'disorderly' but 'idle'. It seems probable that some Thessalonian Christians, believing that the Lord's return was imminent, were playing truant from work. It is these idle Christians whom Paul commands to mind their own affairs, work with their own hands and earn their own living, adding that 'if anyone will not work, let him not eat'.[50]

Before we leave this second principle of Biblical interpretation, another matter must be broached. Since God's revelation was given in a particular historical and geographical situation, this means that it had a particular cultural setting as well. And the social customs which form the background of some Biblical instruction are entirely foreign to those of our day. Are we then to reject the teaching because it is culturally dated? Or are we to go to the other extreme and try to invest both teaching and setting with the same permanent validity? Neither of these seems to be the right way to escape the dilemma. The third and better way is to accept the Biblical instruction itself as permanently binding, but to translate it into contemporary cultural terms. Thus, Jesus commanded His disciples to wash one another's feet as a mark of the mutual love which humbles itself to serve, and the apostles Paul and Peter commanded their readers, when they came together, to greet one another with a holy kiss or a kiss of love.[51] We have no liberty to repudiate these commandments. But nor should we give them a slavishly literal obedience. For nowadays (at least in the west) we do not walk through dusty streets in sandals, and therefore do not need to have our feet washed. Nor is it customary to go round kissing everybody in public. Nevertheless, we can and must obey Christ's injunction through other outward forms of humble service, and obey the apostles' command by 'a handshake all round', as J. B. Phillips

23

aptly paraphrases the kiss of peace. Let it be clear that the purpose of such a cultural transposition is not to avoid obedience, but rather to ensure it.

A more difficult example of the tension between the permanently valid and the culturally dated concerns the status, behaviour and dress of women. Are we to retain all the detailed Biblical requirements, or—in deference to the increasingly vocal 'Women's Lib' movement—jettison the lot? Again there seems to be a wiser middle course. Consider the question of the veiling of women, to which Paul devotes half a chapter in First Corinthians (11). He insists that it is dishonourable, even disgraceful, for a woman to pray or prophesy in public with her head unveiled. He appeals to reason, nature, ecclesiastical custom and his own apostolic authority in support of his teaching. What are we to make of this? Perhaps the commonest and most superficial reaction is to suppose that the apostle's requirement is met if women wear hats in church. But eastern veils and western hats are entirely different, theologically as well as culturally! One of the crucial statements of Paul's argument occurs in verse 10 where, in referring to a woman's duty 'to have a veil on her head' (RSV), he actually writes that she ought to wear 'authority' (RSV margin) on her head. This is the point. In those days the veil the woman wore was a symbol of her husband's authority over her. Not only does a woman's hat not have this significance today, but some modern modes appear to symbolize the exact reverse—liberation, not submission! What is permanently valid in Paul's teaching is the authority of the husband, for he grounds it on unchanging theological truths concerning creation. What is culturally dated is the veil. We must find other social customs which express a woman's acceptance of the authority which God has given to man.

In addition, we must be very careful how we interpret the husband's 'authority'. The word is by no means a synonym for authoritarianism. Nor can it be taken to express any 'superiority' of the male or 'inferiority' of the female. For—centuries in advance of his time—Paul emphatically declared that in Christ 'there is neither male nor female'.[52] He also drew a profound analogy between the relationship of husband and wife in marriage and the relationship between the Father and the Son in the Godhead.[53] This suggests that the husband's 'headship' over his wife is not incompatible with their equality, any more than is the Father's 'headship' over Christ. Perhaps the husband's authority should be understood in terms rather of responsibility than of autocracy, the responsibility of a loving care.

The General Sense

Thirdly, we must look for the *general* sense of Scripture. This is the principle of harmony.

From a human standpoint the Bible is a symposium with a wide assortment of contributors. From the divine standpoint, however, the whole Bible emanates from one mind. It is the word of God expressing the mind of God, and so possesses an organic unity. For this reason we must approach Scripture with the confidence both that God has spoken and that, in speaking, He has not contradicted Himself.

Sir Charles Odgers, in the book mentioned earlier, gives as his seventh rule for interpreting legal documents 'the deed is to be construed as a whole'. He goes on:

'The deed must be read and interpreted as a whole in order to extract the meaning of any particular part or expression . . . Every part of the deed ought to be compared with the other and one entire sense ought to be made thereof . . . Every part of it may be brought into action in order to collect from the whole one uniform and consistent sense, if that may be done. . . .

25

The words of each clause should be so interpreted as to bring them into harmony with the other provisions of the deed if that interpretation does no violence to the meaning of which they are naturally susceptible'.[54]

As with legal documents, so with the Biblical text we should seek to resolve apparent discrepancies and interpret Scripture as one harmonious whole. This will lead us to interpret Scripture by Scripture, especially what is obscure by what is plain, and never so to 'expound one place of Scripture that it be repugnant to another'.[55]

This was John Knox's argument with Mary Queen of Scots. In a private debate with her in Edinburgh in 1561 he asserted that the Church of Rome (which she said she would defend as the true Church of God) had declined from the purity of religion taught by the apostles. The Queen herself, he added, possessed little right knowledge, since she had heard no teachers but those allowed by the Pope and his Cardinals. At this the Queen said:

'Ye interpret the Scriptures in one manner, and they in another; whom shall I believe, and who shall judge?'

John Knox replied:

'Believe God, that plainly speaketh in His Word: And further than the Word teacheth you, ye shall neither believe the one nor the other. The Word of God is plain in itself; And if there appear any obscurity in one place, the Holy Ghost, which is never contrarious to Himself, explains the same more clearly in other places'.[56]

We may say, therefore, that every text of Scripture has a double context, historical and scriptural. Its context in history is the situation in which it was written. Its context in Scripture is the place where it is found. So each text must be understood against both its historical and its scriptural background. These are our second and

26

third principles of interpretation respectively, the principles of history and of harmony.

Further, the scriptural context of every text is both immediate (the paragraph, chapter and book in which it is embedded) and distant (the total Biblical revelation).

The immediate context is the more obvious. To wrench a text from its context is an inexcusable blunder, and many horrific tales are told of preachers who have done it. In his instruction on the local church's responsibility to discipline an impenitent offender, Jesus said: 'if he refuses to hear the church, let him be to you as a Gentile . . .' i.e. let him be excommunicated.[57] Now during the Tractarian movement which sought to restore the Church of England's 'catholic' authority, its followers preached so often on the three words of this verse 'hear the church' that they provoked Archbishop Whately to retort with a sermon on the equally truncated text 'if he refuses to hear the church, let him . . .'!

Perhaps this kind of trickery, which exploits a combination of words without any respect for their true contextual meaning, is so outrageous as to be comparatively rare. Yet I was myself greatly disturbed that the World Council of Churches (which ought to have known better) should take as the text for their Fourth Assembly at Uppsala in 1967 God's great words in Revelation 21.5 'Behold, I make all things new', where the sentence applies to what He is going to do in the end when He makes a new heaven and a new earth, and should then proceed without any conceivable justification to apply it to the political, revolutionary movements of today.

It is in some ways even more important that we should learn to see the Bible as a whole, and to read each text in the light of all. Let me give some examples of what I mean.

To begin with let us look a little more closely at the early chapters of Genesis. Perhaps these chapters are specially susceptible to misunderstanding whenever they are isolated from the rest of Scripture. My own position is to accept the historicity of Adam and Eve, but to remain agnostic about some details of the story like the precise nature of the tree of life and of the serpent. This is not to be arbitrary or inconsistent, however, for I have Biblical reasons for both. That Adam and Eve were literal people seems clear from Romans 5.12–21, where Paul draws a deliberate contrast between the disobedience of Adam through which sin and death entered the world and the obedience of Christ who secured salvation and life. The analogy is meaningless if Adam's act of disobedience was not an event as historical as Christ's act of obedience. But as for the serpent and the tree of life, they both reappear in the *Book of Revelation*, where they are clearly symbolical, the serpent representing Satan and the tree eternal life. So I have a *Biblical* (New Testament) reason for believing that Adam and Eve were historical, and an equally *Biblical* reason for supposing that the serpent and the trees in the story may in some sense be meant to be figurative.

When I was a Cambridge undergraduate, I can remember being rather perplexed by the verse which says that the ten commandments were written on stone tablets by the finger of God.[58] Was I required to believe this literally? Did a divine finger really appear and somehow inscribe Hebrew letters on stone? Certainly it is not impossible, for 'the fingers of a man's hand appeared and wrote on the plaster of the wall of the king's palace' in the case of King Belshazzar, announcing his imminent doom.[59] But today I am not so sure that we were ever meant to take literally the statement about the finger of God writing the law. For now I have read the Bible more thoroughly, and I have come across other references to God's fingers, all of which are symbolical. Thus, David

28

referred to the heavens as the work of God's fingers.[60] Again, after the plague of gnats on man and beast the Egyptian magicians said to Pharaoh 'This is the finger of God', and after Jesus had begun to cast out demons He claimed to do it 'by the finger of God'.[61] If then, the reference to God's finger in the writing of the law is comparable to these other references, it seems that 'the finger of God' is a Biblical figure of speech for God's immediate intervention whether in creation (the heavens), in revelation (the law), in judgment (the plagues) or in salvation (the exorcism of demons). Such an interpretation would be in keeping with the principle of harmony.

Another example of the importance of considering each part of Scripture's teaching on any subject in the light of the whole is the second coming of Christ. It would be easy (and dangerous) to be selective in the texts from which we build up our doctrine. Thus, some passages indicate that Christ's return will be personal and visible, indeed that He will come 'in the same way' as He went.[62] But before we press this into meaning that the Return will be a kind of Ascension in reverse, like a film played backwards, and that Christ will set His feet on the precise spot on the Mount of Olives from which He was taken up, we need to consider something Jesus said to counter those who wanted to localize His return:

'As the lightning flashes and lights up the sky from one side to the other, so will the Son of man be in His day'.[63]

The truly Biblical Christian, anxious to be faithful to all Scripture, will want to do equal justice to both these strands of teaching. The coming of the Lord will indeed be personal, historical and visible; but it will also be 'in power and great glory', as universal as the lightning, a transcendent event of which the whole human population of both hemispheres will be simultaneously aware.

In my last examples of the need to see Scripture as a

29

whole, I want to say something about both the Mosaic law and the fulfilment of prophecy. This will throw light on the relation between the Old and the New Testaments, and so on the question of progressive revelation. The principle of harmony does not deny that there has been progression in God's revelation of Himself and of His purposes, but emphasizes rather that the progression has not been from error to truth, but from truth to more truth.

Take the law of Moses. It is recognised in both Old and New Testaments that Moses' law was God's law. Moses was but the intermediary through whom God gave His law to His people. But does the divine origin of the law mean that it is all still permanently binding on Christian people? No. For Moses' law was a complex code, consisting of moral instructions, ceremonial regulations and civil statutes. The New Testament clearly teaches that the *ceremonial* rules are now obsolete, the temple, priesthood and sacrifices having been fulfilled in Christ and the food laws having been abolished by Him.[64] The *civil* laws of Moses still have importance as indications of divine righteousness and justice, but no church or nation is under obligation to enact and enforce them today. There are several reasons for this. For one thing, the civil code of Moses was framed for a people who belonged to God by redemption; they were both a nation and a church simultaneously, whereas today no church is a nation and no nation a church. For another, it was adapted to an emergent nation, who were first a nomadic and then an agricultural community. The *moral* laws of Moses, however, have not been abrogated. On the contrary, they are still in force. Christ died that the righteous requirement of the law might be fulfilled in us, and the Holy Spirit writes God's law in our hearts.[65] Article VII of the Church of England's *Thirty-Nine Articles* sums up these distinctions well:

'Although the laws given from God by Moses, as touching ceremonies and rites, do not bind Christian men, nor the civil precepts thereof ought of necessity to be received in any commonwealth; yet notwithstanding, no Christian man whatsoever is free from the obedience of the commandments which are called moral.'

We turn now from law to prophecy. The great conviction of the New Testament authors is that with Jesus Christ the 'last days' foretold throughout the Old Testament had come, and that in Him and in His people the great promises of God found their fulfilment. Paul could even claim before King Agrippa:

'I stand here testifying both to small and great, saying nothing but what the prophets and Moses said would come to pass . . .'.[66]

There is some disagreement among Biblical Christians as to whether we are to expect the Old Testament promises about Israel's future to be literally fulfilled, and whether the modern state of Israel in its occupation of the Holy Land is at least a partial fulfilment of them. Certainly God has a great future for the Jews, which is figuratively set forth by Paul as the grafting back into their own olive tree of the natural branches which had been broken off.[67] But there is no mention in the New Testament of any literal return of the Jews to the promised land. The overwhelming emphasis of the New Testament is that the Christian Church is now 'the Israel of God', 'the true circumcision', 'a chosen race, a royal priesthood, a holy nation, God's own people',[68] and that God's great promises to Abraham of both a posterity and a land are fulfilled spiritually in Christ and His Church:

'So you see that it is men of faith who are sons of

31

Abraham . . . Those who are men of faith are blessed with Abraham who had faith.'
'Christ redeemed us from the curse of the law, having become a curse for us . . . that in Christ Jesus the blessing of Abraham might come upon the Gentiles, that we might receive the promise of the Spirit through faith.'
'If you are Christ's, then you are Abraham's offspring, heirs according to promise.'[69]

To be more precise, the fulfilment of Old Testament prophecy is usually in three stages. First came an immediate or literal fulfilment. The second stage, in which we are living, is the gospel or spiritual fulfilment. One day will come the third stage, which will be the final or heavenly fulfilment. Thus, the promise to Abraham of an innumerable posterity was historically fulfilled in the children of Israel,[70] is being fulfilled today in Christ's people, and will be consummated in heaven in the 'great multitude which no man could number' round God's throne.[71] Or again, the Old Testament prophets predicted the rebuilding of the temple, and there was an immediate and literal rebuilding under Zerubbabel. Today, however, it is the Christian Church which is 'a holy temple in the Lord, . . . a dwelling place of God in the Spirit',[72] and so is the individual Christian's body also.[73] In the new or heavenly Jerusalem, however, there will be no separate temple, 'for its temple is the Lord God the Almighty and the Lamb' dwelling in the midst of His people for evermore.[74]

*   *   *

In conclusion, let me emphasize that the three principles of Biblical interpretation we have been considering are not arbitrary. They are derived from the character of the Bible itself as God's word written.

We look for the *natural* meaning because we believe

that God intended His revelation to be a plain and readily intelligible communication to ordinary human beings.

We look for the *original* meaning because we believe that God addressed His word to those who first heard it, and that it can be received by subsequent generations only in so far as they understand it historically. Our understanding may be fuller than that of the first hearers (e.g. of the prophecies of Christ); it cannot be substantially different.

We look for the *general* meaning because we believe that God is self-consistent, and that His revelation is self-consistent also.

So our three principles (of simplicity, history and harmony) arise partly from the nature of God and partly from the nature of Scripture as a plain, historical, consistent communication from God to men. They lay upon us a solemn responsibility to make our treatment of Scripture coincide with our view of it.

For Further Reading

Understanding God's Word by the Rev. Alan M. Stibbs (IVF 1950, 64 pages). The author was a gifted Bible expositor and for many years Vice-Principal of Oak Hill Theological College, London. He lists the rules—both 'general' and 'special'—for interpreting the text of Scripture. A wise, balanced and suggestive little book.

A Christian's Guide to Bible Study by A. Morgan Derham (Hodder & Stoughton 1963, 63 pages). The author writes from the conviction 'that straightforward Bible study is possible for the ordinary Christian', and indeed as exciting as it is neglected. After some introductory material on the Bible's authority and purpose, he lists six 'Basic Principles' to guide the reader in his interpretation, and goes on to give practical suggestions on both methods of study (with some concrete examples) and the necessary tools.

Principles of Biblical Interpretation by Louis Berkhof
(Baker Book House 1950, 169 pages). A rather
technical but very thorough treatment by the former
President of Calvin Seminary, Grand Rapids. After
introductory chapters on the history of interpretation
among the Jews and in the Church, and on the inspiration, unity, diversity and style of Scripture, the
author elaborates three basic principles of interpretation – grammatical, historical and theological. A
textbook for preachers and teachers.

NOTES

1 2 Pet. 1.21
2 Is. 29.11, 12
3 Jn. 3.3
4 1 Cor. 2.14
5 *Five Christian Leaders of
the Eighteenth Century*
by Bishop J. C. Ryle,
first published 1868.
Banner of Truth edition
1960 p. 28
6 Mt. 11.25, 26
7 J. J. Gurney's memoir
of an afternoon spent in
Cambridge with Simeon
in 1831, recorded in
*Memoirs of the Life of
the Rev. Charles Simeon*
edited by William Carus
(Hatchard 1847) p. 674
8 Ps. 119.18
9 Eph. 1.17–19 cf. 3.14–19;
Phil. 1.9–11 and Col.
1.9–14
10 *George Whitefield's
Journals*, first published
between 1738 and 1741.

Banner of Truth edition
1960, p. 60
11 2 Tim. 3.15
12 Jn. 7.17; 14.21
13 1 Tim. 1.19
14 Mk. 4.21–25
15 Ps. 32.9
16 e.g. Mk. 8.17–21
17 Lk. 12.57
18 1 Cor. 3.16; 5.6; 6.2, 3,
9, 15, 16, 19
19 e.g. 1 Cor. 10.1; 12.1
20 1 Cor. 2.14–16
21 1 Cor. 10.15 cf. 11.13
22 1 Jn. 4.1
23 Rom. 14.5
24 Heb. 5.14
25 Dan. 10.12
26 2 Tim. 2.7
27 sermon 975 in *Horae
Homileticae*. 1819
28 Recorded in Foxe's
Book of Martyrs Vol. IV
29 Eph. 3.18, 19
30 Eph. 4.11, 12
31 Col. 3.16

32 Commentary on Acts
    8.31 in the Oliver and
    Boyd edition p. 247
33 Mt. 23.8–10
34 Is. 54.13; Jn. 6.45; 1
    Thess. 1.9
35 1 Jn. 2.15–27
36 Ps. 119.99
37 Acts 17.11
38 2 Cor. 4.2; 2 Pet. 3.16
39 1 Jn. 1.5
40 *The Construction of
    Deeds and Statutes.*
    First published by Sweet
    and Maxwell in 1939.
    Fourth Edition 1956 p.27
41 *The Apostolic Fathers*
    edited by J. B. Lightfoot.
    Macmillan 1891 p. 279
42 Comment on Galatians
    4.22. William Pringle's
    translation (Calvin
    Translation Society)
    1854 p. 136
43 Jn. 3.3, 4; 4.10–15; 6.51,
    52
44 Lk. 10.29–37
45 Rev. 7.14
46 The italics are Simeon's.
    The quotation comes
    from a letter to his
    publisher Mr. Holdsworth
    (undated, although
    apparently 1832) in
    *Memoirs of the Life of
    the Rev. Charles Simeon*
    (edited by William Carus.
    Hatchard 1847 2nd
    edition p. 703)
47 *What is Faith?* by J.
    Gresham Machen 1st
    published 1925. Hodder
    edition (undated) p. 24
48 Rom. 3.28; 4.1–3
49 Jas. 2.21–24
50 1 Thess. 4.11; 5.14; 2
    Thess. 3.6–12
51 Jn. 13.12–17; Rom.
    16.16; 2 Cor. 13.12; 1
    Thess. 5.26; 1 Pet. 5.14
52 Gal. 3.28
53 1 Cor. 11.3
54 *ibid.* p. 39
55 Article XX *Of the
    Authority of the Church*
    from the Church of
    England's Thirty-nine
    Articles
56 The debate is recorded
    near the beginning of
    Book 4 of *The History
    of the Reformation of the
    Church of Scotland* by
    John Knox. Unfinished
    edition 1587. 1st
    complete edition 1644
    p. 314
57 Mt. 18.17
58 Ex. 31.18; Deut. 9.10
59 Dan. 5.5, 24–28
60 Ps. 8.3
61 Ex. 8.19; Lk. 11.20
62 Acts 1.11
63 Lk. 17.24 cf. Mt. 24.27
64 Consider the use of the
    words 'shadow' and
    'copy' in Heb. 8.5; 9.24;
    10.1 and Mark's
    editorial comment in
    7.19
65 Rom. 8.3, 4; Jer. 31.33
    cf. 2 Cor. 3.6–8
66 Acts 26.22
67 Rom. 11.13–27

68 Gal. 6.16; Phil. 3.3; 1
   Pet. 2.9
69 Gal. 3.7, 9, 13, 14, 29 cf.
   Rom. 4.13, 16. In verse
   13 God's promise to
   Abraham and his
   descendants is 'that they
   should inherit the
   world'. cf. 1 Cor. 3.21–23
70 cf. Num. 23.10; 1
   Kings 4.20
71 Rev. 7.9

72 Eph. 2.21, 22; cf. 1 Cor.
   3.16. Consider also how
   James saw in the
   Gentiles' inclusion in the
   Church a fulfilment of
   God's promise through
   Amos to rebuild the
   ruins of David's dwelling.
   Acts 15.13–18; Amos
   9.11, 12
73 1 Cor. 6.19, 20
74 Rev. 21.3, 22

THE USE OF THE BIBLE

Basic to our Christian faith is the conviction that our God, far from being dead and dumb, is living and vocal. He has spoken a precise message in a precise historical and geographical context, and has caused it to be written and preserved in the Bible. Moreover, as we have considered, there are sound reasons for accepting the Bible's authority and sound principles to guide us in its interpretation.

So what? Why have we spent so much time on these matters? For one reason only, that God still speaks through what He has spoken. What He said centuries ago has a vital relevance to contemporary men and women. The Bible is not an antique piece whose proper home is a museum. On the contrary, it is a 'lamp' to our feet and a 'light' to our path.[1] God's words can be our 'counsellors' in all the perplexities of modern life. They give wisdom and understanding to the simple.[2]

But whether we derive any benefit from Scripture depends on how we use it, on what response we make to its message. One of God's recurring complaints in the Biblical record itself is that His people continually turned a deaf ear to His word. His messengers had to keep pleading with Israel:

'O that today you would hearken to His voice!'[3]

There are in the end only two possible attitudes to God's word, to receive it or to reject it. Those who are receptive to it are portrayed with vivid figures of speech. They are said to 'tremble' at it, just because it is the word of the great God Himself.[4] They prize it like gold and relish it like honey.[5] They rejoice over it 'like one who finds great spoil'. They thirst for it with the ardour of a suckled child.[6] On the other hand those who reject it are said to have closed their ears and refused to listen, 'stiffening their neck' and following 'the stubbornness of their evil heart'.[7] Of such there is no more notorious example than King Jehoiakim, who, as the scroll of God's words through Jeremiah was read to him, first used a penknife to cut it into pieces and then threw the pieces into the fire until the whole scroll had been burned.[8]

Jesus similarly warned His contemporaries about their response to His teaching. In the Parable of the Sower the different soils into which the seed fell were intended to exemplify the varying reception which people give God's word. Jesus solemnly insisted that we shall be judged on the last day by the word He has spoken.[9] All of us are building our life on some foundation. Those who build on rock, whose house will survive the storms of adversity and of judgment, are those who listen to Christ's teaching and put it into practice.[10]

To begin with, to listen involves time. Do we really believe that *God* has spoken, that *God's* words are recorded in Scripture, and that as we read it we may hear *God's* voice addressing us? Then we shall not grudge the time to listen. Instead, we shall want to register our protest against the rat-race of twentieth-century life and strive to recover the lost art of meditation. It is not a casual, superficial acquaintance with Scripture that the modern Church needs, but rather to heed our Master's exhortation:

'Let these words sink into your ears.'[11]

There is no particular secret about how to do it. It just takes time, purposefully redeemed from our busy lives, in which to turn Scripture over and over in our minds until it sinks into our hearts and so regulates everything we think and do. It is those who thus 'meditate day and night' in God's word whom He pronounces 'blessed'.[12]

If there is no single secret, there are no hard and fast rules either. For example, the practice of the daily 'Quiet Time' of Bible reading and prayer, preferably first thing in the morning and last thing at night, is not an inviolable tradition. It has certainly stood the test of time and brought untold profit to many generations of Christians. I am myself old-fashioned enough to retain confidence in it as an extremely valuable discipline. But it is still only a tradition; it has not been laid down in Scripture. So we have no liberty to add it to the decalogue as a kind of eleventh commandment. Nor was such a practice possible before the invention of printing and the availability of cheap Bibles for all. To insist on it as indispensable to Christian living would be to disqualify the millions of Christians who lived in the first fifteen centuries.

The great value of some Scripture meditation and prayer (however brief) at the beginning of each day is that it prepares us to bear the day's responsibilities and face the day's temptations. It seems unwise, to say the least, to go into the conflict unarmed. Nevertheless, the mother who has to cook the breakfast, and then get husband off to work and children off to school, may have to postpone her time with God until later in the morning, while the breadwinner who leaves home very early may prefer to requisition a little time from his (or her) lunch break.

However busy one's daily timetable may be, the increasing numbers who work a five-day week should be able to devote a longer time to Bible reading and prayer over the week-end. Sunday afternoon has obvious possibilities, or even Sunday evening since there is nothing in Scripture requiring Christians to attend church twice every Sunday! Further, if daily family prayers are impossible from Monday to Friday because work and school demand staggered meal-times, a weekly time when the family honours God together in their home, whatever form it takes, should be possible during the weekend.

It is not only by personal or family Bible reading that we can hear God's word, however. It is also through group Bible studies, whether organized by the local church or by a Christian Union or by ourselves in our own home, and (above all) through the public exposition of Scripture in church. I wish modern Christians took this more seriously. It is easy to blame the pulpit, but very often the pew gets the kind of pulpit ministry it wants. God said to Jeremiah:

> 'An appalling and horrible thing has happened in the land: the prophets prophesy falsely, and the priests rule at their direction; *My people love to have it so.* . . .'[13]

Congregations have far more responsibility than they commonly recognize for the kind of ministry they receive. They should encourage their minister to expound Scripture. They should come to church in a receptive and expectant mood, preferably bringing their Bible with them, hungry to hear what the Lord God may have to say to them through the lessons and the sermon. It may also be wise to take some steps to retain the message in their memory, perhaps by writing the text on a card and then meditating on it during the rest of the week. And if the church we attend is not blessed with a ministry of Biblical exposition, the modern cassette recorder has brought the ministry of other Bible teachers within reach of many people, for personal or group listening.

Precisely how the individual Christian or the Christian family seeks to receive the message of the Bible is not the most important question. What is vital is that in some way at some time, and that regularly, we learn to listen to God's word and to feed upon it in our hearts.

This listening to God's voice in and through His word is only the beginning, however. It is not enough to 'know these things', Jesus said; we shall be blessed only if we 'do them'.[14] For according to the New Testament the truth is something to be 'done', not merely 'known'.[15] Perhaps no apostle put this more clearly than James, the Lord's brother, who wrote:

'But be doers of the word, and not hearers only, deceiving yourselves.'[16]

To 'do' the truth is to do what it says, to translate its message into action. This sounds simple, but it has far-reaching implications simply because the truth we have to 'do' is so rich. Let me give five facets of the life-style of a 'doer of the word'.

Worship

First, worship. Worship is impossible without a knowledge of the truth. I grant that Paul found an altar in Athens which was inscribed 'to an unknown God'. But it is ludicrous to try to worship a deity we do not know, for if we do not know Him we do not know what kind of worship He desires. Conversely, once we have even begun to know the living and true God, we must worship Him. And the more we come to know Him, the more we shall realise that He is worthy of our devotion. For to worship is to praise God's name, to glory in who and what He is in the splendour of His being and His works:

'Let them praise the name of the Lord, for His name alone is exalted; His glory is above earth and heaven.'[17]

Since worship is always a response to the truth of God we perceive, it is supremely the word of God (His self-revelation) which evokes the worship of God. Therefore the Bible has an indispensable place in both public and private worship. In all public worship there should be a reading (or readings) of Scripture, and an exhortation or instruction based on it.[18] Far from being an intrusion into the service, both are essential to worship. So those who have the privilege of reading lessons in church should take pains to understand the passage, and those who are called to preach should be conscientious in studying both God's word and man's world in order to relate the one to the other. Only when God speaks through His word, making Himself known in the greatness of His glory and grace, do the congregation truly bow down and worship.

The same principle applies to private devotion. Apart from a humble prayer for illumination, we should worship and pray *after* our Bible reading. For it is from Scripture that we shall learn whom to worship and how to pray according to God's will.[19]

Repentance and Faith

The second mark of a 'doer of the word' is repentance. For God's word tells us what *we* are as well as what *He* is, discloses to us our sin, and calls us to confess and forsake it. Several of the graphic similes of Scripture enforce this truth. The word of God is like a mirror, showing us what we are like,[20] like a sword to prick our guilty conscience,[21] and like both a hammer and a fire to

42

break and purify us.[22] Whenever we read the Scripture we hear God saying to us:

'Thus says the Lord of hosts. . . . "Amend your ways and your doings. . . . Remove the evil of your doings from before My eyes; cease to do evil, learn to do good. . . ." '[23]

The third characteristic of the 'doer of the word' is faith. Faith is an integral part of the Christian life, for 'without faith it is impossible to please' God.[24] Christians are frequently described in the New Testament as 'believers' who 'through faith and patience inherit the promises'.[25] But faith is very commonly misunderstood. It is not screwing ourselves up to believe something which we strongly suspect is not true; it is resting confidently on Him who is true. Faith cannot exist in a vacuum or in isolation; it is always a trustful response to a trustworthy person. We must never set faith and knowledge over against one another as if they were mutually exclusive. For faith is based on knowledge:

'Those who know Thy name put their trust in Thee.'[26]

We trust God because we know Him to be trustworthy. How? Because He has revealed Himself to be such. As we read in Scripture about the character and mighty deeds of God, about His faithfulness to His covenant in the history of Israel, about 'His precious and very great promises',[27] about Jesus Christ in whom all God's promises find their 'yes',[28] and about the men of faith who were 'fully convinced that God was able to do what He had promised',[29] our faith is quickened, nourished and matured.

So then it is no use moaning that we seem to suffer from a chronic unbelief, or envying others ('I wish I had your faith'), as if our lack of faith were like our temperament, a congenital condition which cannot be changed.

For God himself has given us the means to increase our faith:

'Faith comes from what is heard, and what is heard comes by the preaching of Christ.'[30]

We have to take time and trouble to hear in order to believe. The Christian who wants to grow in faith must spend time meditating on God's word. He will soon discover what is meant by 'the encouragement of the Scriptures'.[31]

Obedience

Obedience is the fourth way by which we become 'doers' of the word and not only 'hearers'. Yet obedience involves submission to authority, and this is out of fashion today. However, if Jesus Christ Himself lived in humble obedience to God's word, obeying its commands as well as believing its promises, there can be no doubt that we must also. For the servant is not greater than his master.

Jesus went further than that. He indicated that, just as ancient Israel was to prove her love for God by obeying Him, so Christian disciples must prove their love for Christ by their obedience:

'If you love Me, you will keep my commandments . . . He who has My commandments and keeps them, he it is who loves Me . . . If a man loves Me, he will keep My word . . . he who does not love Me does not keep My words'.[32]

It seems to me that we should be more grateful to God than we customarily are that He has revealed His will so clearly on so many subjects in His word. For the very first step towards holiness of life is a knowledge of what is pleasing and displeasing to God.[33] So the Christian's dearest ambition is 'to live according to Scripture',[34] for

44

there is no other way to be sure of living according to His will.

This goes for social as well as personal righteousness. For the will of God in the word of God for the people of God relates to the whole of our lives. It tells us to love God, to control ourselves and to love and serve our neighbour. And the requirement of neighbour-love has many and wide ramifications. For my neighbour has a body as well as a soul, and lives by God's ordering in a community. So I cannot claim to love him if I ignore either his physical or his social well-being.

We have already seen with what detailed applications the Hebrew prophets proclaimed the righteousness of God. The home, the market place, the law-court, the farm—these were the places where righteousness was to be practised. And where it was lacking, there the judgment of God would fall. The prophets were fearless in thundering their woes upon the unrighteous, upon the trader who cheated his customers by using false weights and measures, upon the greedy landowner who joined house to house and field to field until there was no more room, upon the magistrate who perverted justice by taking bribes from the guilty rich and condemning the innocent poor, upon the husband who profaned the divine institutions of marriage and home by his sexual unfaithfulness, upon the moneylender who charged extortionate rates of interest, even upon the king who oppressed the people instead of serving them. And by contrast the Book of Proverbs, full of practical wisdom, extols the virtues of honesty, industry, generosity, humility, chastity and justice.

The apostles too, in the ethical sections of their letters, lay great stress on social righteousness. They portray what should be the mutual relations between husband and wife, parents and children, employers and employees. Paul exposes the gravity of tolerating in the Christian community such sins as factions due to a personality cult, litigation and immorality. The liar is to learn to speak the truth, and the thief to earn his own living so that he can give to those in need. All bitterness, anger, slander and malice are to be put away. Christians are to be kind, tender-hearted, forbearing, tolerant, and even (as Jesus taught) to love and serve their enemies. James inveighs against class distinctions in the Christian fellowship, against our unruly tongues, and against jealousy and selfish ambition. In the last chapter of his letter he sounds just like an Old Testament prophet as he condemns the rich for their luxurious living and their fraudulent treatment of their own farm labourers.

It is true that there are many complex ethical questions of the modern world on which Scripture does not directly pronounce. But the principles are there on which we must form a responsible Christian judgment. Whether the issue is war or violent revolution, pollution, pornography or poverty, or political and economic theory, we cannot escape the labour—and sometimes the pain—of seeking to formulate a Biblically-conditioned Christian opinion.

Witness

The fifth mark of a Christian who 'does' God's word is witness. For truth cannot be concealed or monopolized. If our eyes have been opened to receive it, we know ourselves under compulsion to pass it on. We are 'stewards of the mysteries of God',[35] trustees of His secrets. Not only must we bear witness to the Christ we have come to know, but we cannot bear witness without this knowledge.

The words 'witness' and 'testimony' have been much devalued, and are sometimes employed to describe what is little more than an essay in religious autobiography.

But Christian witness is witness to Christ. And the Christ to whom we have a responsibility to witness is not merely the Christ of our personal experience, but the historic Christ, the Christ of the apostolic testimony. There is no other Christ. So if Scripture leads to witness, witness also depends on Scripture.

The Bible, then, has an essential place in the life of a Christian. For the revelation of God leads to worship, the warnings of God to repentance, the promises of God to faith, the commands of God to obedience and the truth of God to witness. It is no exaggeration to say that without Scripture a Christian life is impossible. True, there are still many in the world who are illiterate, and cannot read the Bible. Others can read, but do not or not much, either because of their cultural background or because of the electronic revolution or because of some innate reluctance. Is a Christian life to be denied to them? No, of course not. If (for whatever reason) they do not read Scripture and meditate on it by themselves, I am bound to say I think they will be spiritually impoverished. But they can certainly receive God's word in other ways as I have indicated earlier—through sermons, through group study, through the mass media and through person-to-person communication.

Nevertheless, God's word is indispensable to us, by whatever means we receive it. Jesus Himself put this beyond question when He quoted from Deuteronomy:

'Man shall not live by bread alone, but by every word that proceeds from the mouth of God.'[36]

God's word is as essential to us spiritually as food is to us physically. Both life and health are—quite literally—impossible without it. It is by His word that God implants spiritual life within us.[37] It is by the same word that He instructs, reforms, nourishes, encourages and

47

strengthens us. It is truly by His word alone that the man of God grows into maturity and becomes 'equipped for every good work'.[38]

For Further Reading

Live a New Life by David Watson (Inter-Varsity Press 1975, 78 pages). All God's true children *have* new life. But how do we set about *living* this new life? In this readable practical book David Watson delineates the various aspects of Christian experience and service. He includes sections on vital questions such as doubt.

Profiting from the Word by A. W. Pink (Banner of Truth Trust 1970, 124 pages). This book outlines the principles and methods which can make Bible study rewarding. Among the subjects included are: the Scriptures, Sin, God, Christ, Prayer, Good Works, Obedience, the World, the Promises, Joy and Love.

Holiness by J. C. Ryle (James Clarke edition 1952, 333 pages). John Charles Ryle, the first and evangelical bishop of Liverpool at the end of the last century, brought together in this volume twenty papers on practical, scriptural holiness, 'its nature, hindrances, difficulties and roots'. He was deeply concerned by what he regarded as the unscriptural notions popular in his day, and pleads here for an informed, balanced, wholehearted response to the teaching of Scripture. A spiritual classic which, in my judgment, all Christians should read and absorb.

Learning to Use Your Bible by Oscar E. Feucht (Concordia 1970, 177 pages). The author is an American Lutheran who has had wide experience in both parish ministry and Christian education. The first half of his book contains a fund of practical advice about reading and studying the Bible, both alone and with others. The second half gives information about the Bible's nature, interpretation and contents. It ends with

'thumbnail sketches' of all the Biblical books, and a
chart of the Old Testament.

NOTES

1 Ps. 119.105 c.f. 2 Pet. 1.19
2 Ps. 119.24, 30; Ps. 19.7
3 Ps. 95.7
4 Is. 66.2, 5; Ezra 9.4
5 Ps. 19.10; 119.103, 127
6 Ps. 119.162; 1 Pet. 2.2
7 e.g. Jer. 17.23; 18.12;
  19.15
8 Jer. 36.21–23
9 Jn. 12.47, 48
10 Mt. 7.24–27
11 Lk. 9.44
12 Ps. 1.1, 2; Ps. 119.97;
  Josh. 1.8
13 Jer. 5.30, 31
14 Jn. 13.17
15 e.g. 1 Jn. 1.6 literally
16 Js. 1.22
17 Ps. 148.13
18 cf. Neh. 8.8; 1 Tim. 4.13
19 1 Jn. 5.14; Jn. 15.7
20 Js. 1.23–25
21 Eph. 6.17; Heb. 4.12;
  Acts 2.37
22 Jer. 23.29
23 Jer. 7.3; Is. 1.16, 18
24 Heb. 11.6
25 Heb. 6.12
26 Ps. 9.10
27 2 Pet. 1.4
28 2 Cor. 1.20
29 Rom. 4.21
30 Rom. 10.17
31 Rom. 15.4
32 Jn. 14. 15, 21, 23, 24
33 cf. 1 Thess. 4.1
34 1 Cor. 4.6
35 1 Cor. 4.1
36 Mt. 4.4 quoting Deut.
  8.3
37 Js. 1.21; 1 Pet. 1.23–25
38 2 Tim. 3.17

Have you seen
The Scripture Union
KEY BOOKS
Range?

UNDERSTANDING CHRISTIAN ATTITUDES
George Hoffman

The author deals positively and clearly with the Christian approach to a wide number of social and moral problems.

UNDERSTANDING THE SUPERNATURAL
Canon Stafford Wright

A timely assessment of the occult based on the warnings given in the Bible and the Christian's understanding of the power of Christ and the nature of evil.

UNDERSTANDING THE TEN COMMANDMENTS
John Eddison

The author considers the relevance of the Ten Commandments to contemporary life.

UNDERSTANDING OURSELVES
John Eddison

A sympathetic, Christian view of the anxiety and depression that trouble so many in today's world.

UNDERSTANDING THE WAY
Robinson and Winward

A practical guide to the Christian life.

UNDERSTANDING CHRISTIAN ETHICS
Gilbert Kirby

The principal of the London Bible College considers the application of Christian teaching in dealing with contemporary problems from euthanasia to pornography.

UNDERSTANDING BASIC BELIEFS
John Eddison

An outline of what Christians believe based on one of the great creeds of the Christian church.

LET'S TALK IT THROUGH
J. Hills Cotterill

Discussion starters and background material on a variety of topics from contemporary portrayals of Jesus Christ to the use of music in worship. A mine of information.

UNDERSTANDING LEADERSHIP
John Eddison

Ten studies on 'top men' of the Bible which aim to show exactly what the qualities are that make up a leader.

UNDERSTANDING GOD'S PLAN
David Howard

A very readable commentary on the great themes of the book of Job and their message for us in today's world.

UNDERSTANDING THE DEATH OF JESUS
John Eddison

A lively challenging look at the reasons why Jesus died on the cross and the implications of his death for us today.

UNDERSTANDING THE CHRISTIAN AND SEX
M. O. Vincent

A trained psychiatrist explores the role of sex in the life of the world and of the individual Christian.

DAILY BIBLE STUDY BOOKS

Thorough coverage of major Biblical passages combines scholarly insight with devotional warmth and practical experience. Studies of Biblical characters are also included.

Man separated from God	A. Skevington Wood
	E. M. Blaiklock
Jesus' Early Life	H. L. Ellison
	E. M. Blaiklock
Jesus' True Identity	James Philip
	E. M. Blaiklock
Man restored in Christ	W. L. Lane
	E. M. Blaiklock
God the Holy Spirit	Leon Morris
	E. M. Blaiklock
Christ Living with Him	J. I. Packer
	E. M. Blaiklock
God's Kingdom and Church	F. F. Bruce
	E. M. Blaiklock
Christ the Way to God	R. A. Finlayson
	E. M. Blaiklock

UNDERSTANDING THE NEW TESTAMENT

Based on Scripture Union's popular *Daily Bible Commentary* in four volumes these ten books offer a unique combination of daily Bible readings with the depth of a commentary.

St Matthew	F. F. Bruce
St Mark	I. H. Marshall
St Luke	E. M. Blaiklock
St John	R. E. Nixon
Acts	R. P. Martin
Romans	E. M. Blaiklock
1 Corinthians—Galatians	R. P.Martin
Ephesians—2 Thessalonians	W. L. Lane
1 Timothy—James	Leon Morris
1 Peter—Revelation	H. L. Ellison

SCRIPTURE UNION BIBLE DICTIONARIES

DICTIONARY OF BIBLE WORDS
John Eddison

John Eddison looks at a range of Bible words that are unfamiliar in everyday English and explains their original meaning and modern significance.

DICTIONARY OF BIBLE TIMES
Herbert Sundemo

With the help of maps, charts and over 200 line drawings the author covers, in one handy volume, topics ranging from geography to religious customs.

DICTIONARY OF BIBLE PEOPLE
J. Stafford Wright

Over 500 entries covering the major characters in the Bible. All the relevant facts of their lives are detailed and discussed in a lively, memorable style.

Your Own Personal Notes

55

Your Own Personal Notes